Fully Reproducible Blacklin[es]

BOOK TWO

PHONIC FOLD-UPS

Fun activities to introduce and reinforce phonic sounds

ISBN 1-86400-262-X

9 781864 002621

Prim-Ed Publishing

Phonic Fold-Ups - Book 2
Prim-Ed Publishing

Published in 1996 by Prim-Ed Publishing.

ISBN 1 86400 262 X
PR - 2052

Prim-Ed Publishing Pty. Ltd.
Offices in: United Kingdom: PO Box 051, Nuneaton, Warwickshire, CV11 6ZU
Australia: PO Box 332, Greenwood, Western Australia, 6024
Republic of Ireland: PO Box 8, New Ross, County Wexford, Ireland

• IMPORTANT •

For your added protection in the case of copyright inspection, please complete the form below. Retain this form, the complete original document and the invoice or receipt as proof of purchase.

Name of Purchaser: ______________________

Date of purchase: ______________________

School O/N (if applicable): ______________________

Supplier: ______________________

Signature of purchaser: ______________________

PHONIC FOLD-UPS

BOOK TWO

Published by Prim-Ed Publishing

Foreword

Phonic Fold-Ups is a series of three books designed to make phonics interesting and enjoyable. The books take the children through a series of two and three-letter blends, which can occur at the beginning and the end of a word. The activities are designed to introduce and reinforce particular phonic sounds.

Contents

Teacher Information

The following is a development plan using one of the pages in this book. It is an example of how the activities in this book could be introduced, developed and extended.

Introducing Work

Introduce the children to the phonic sounds 'ung' and 'ang' giving some examples of words which explain these sounds. Encourage discussion and brainstorming in which children are required to offer other words which may have these sounds.

Development

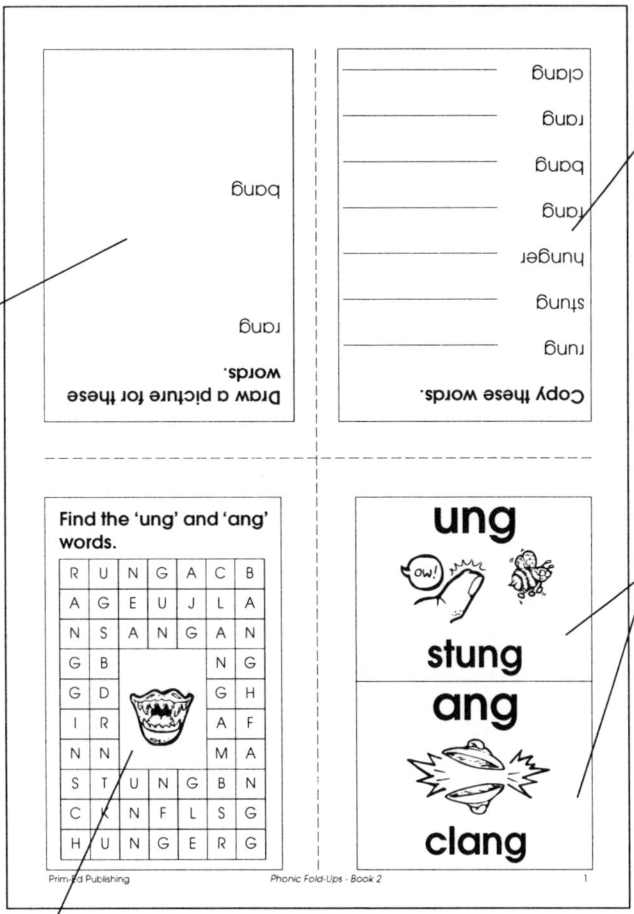

1. Children fold along the dotted line to make a book.

2. (a) Discuss with the children how this sound looks and sounds.
   (b) Children can circle the 'ung' sound in the word stung and the 'ang' sound in the word clang.

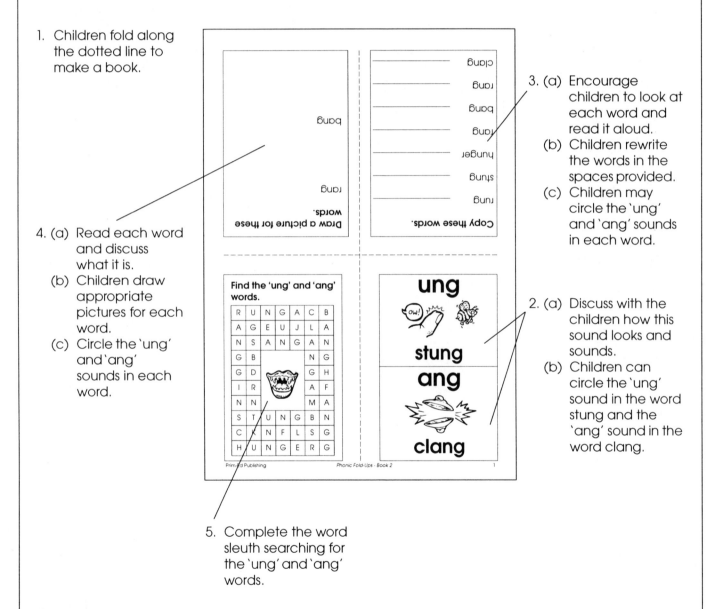

3. (a) Encourage children to look at each word and read it aloud.
   (b) Children rewrite the words in the spaces provided.
   (c) Children may circle the 'ung' and 'ang' sounds in each word.

4. (a) Read each word and discuss what it is.
   (b) Children draw appropriate pictures for each word.
   (c) Circle the 'ung' and 'ang' sounds in each word.

5. Complete the word sleuth searching for the 'ung' and 'ang' words.

Extension

Once children complete the phonic booklet, they may be encouraged to write sentences on their own using the 'ung' and 'ang' words.
The fold-a-book can also be used as a home reader to reinforce the phonic sounds studied in class.

Draw a picture for these words.

rang

bang

Copy these words.

rung ______________

stung ______________

hunger ______________

fang ______________

bang ______________

rang ______________

clang ______________

Find the 'ung' and 'ang' words.

R	U	N	G	A	C	B
A	G	E	U	J	L	A
N	S	A	N	G	A	N
G	B				N	G
G	D				G	H
I	R				A	F
N	N				M	A
S	T	U	N	G	B	N
C	K	N	F	L	S	G
H	U	N	G	E	R	G

ung

stung

ang

clang

Copy these words.

clang ______________________

rang ______________________

bang ______________________

fang ______________________

hunger ______________________

stung ______________________

rung ______________________

Draw a picture for these words.

bang

rang

ung

stung

ang

clang

Find the 'ung' and 'ang' words.

R	U	N	G	A	C	B
A	G	E	U	J	L	A
N	S	A	N	G	A	N
G	B				N	G
G	D				G	H
I	R				A	F
N	N				M	A
S	T	U	N	G	B	N
C	K	N	F	L	S	G
H	U	N	G	E	R	G

Unjumble the 'ing' words.

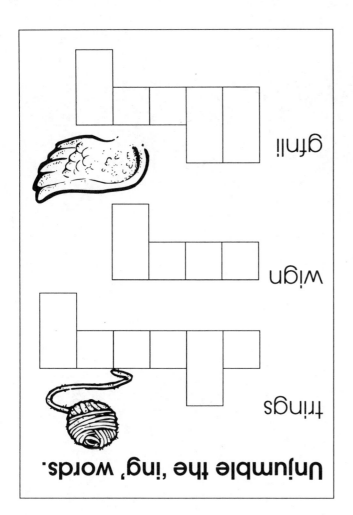

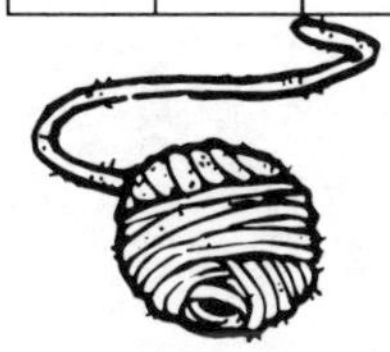

trings

wign

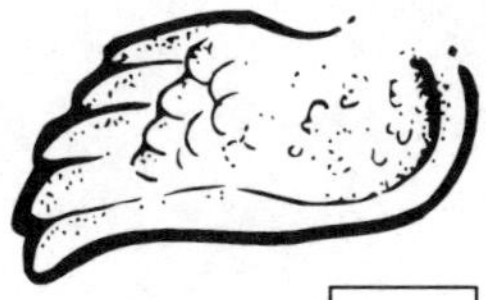

gfnli

Copy these words.

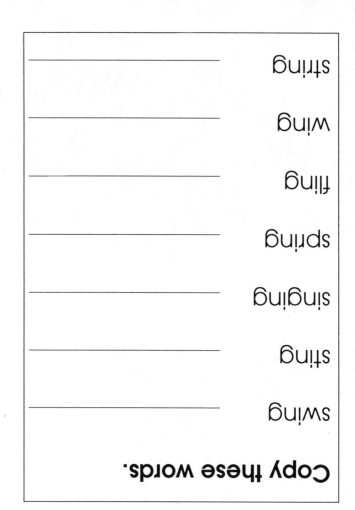

swing ______________

sting ______________

singing ______________

spring ______________

fling ______________

wing ______________

string ______________

Draw a boy on a swing in spring.

ing

ring

Complete each 'ank' words.

th ___ ___ ___

p ___ ___ nk

t ___ ___ k

c ___ ___ ___ k

p ___ ___ nk

___ ___ ___ k

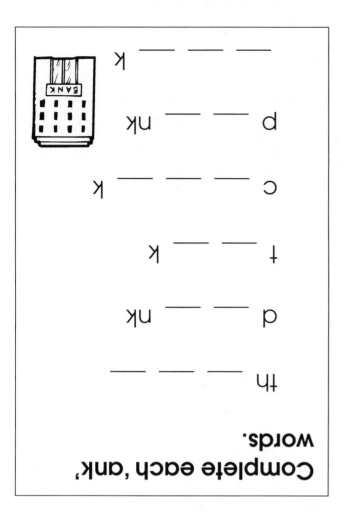

Copy these words.

bank __________

tank __________

crank __________

sank __________

thank __________

spank __________

plank __________

Find and colour the 'ank' words.

banklmandtankmm

wpothanklopkndranklw

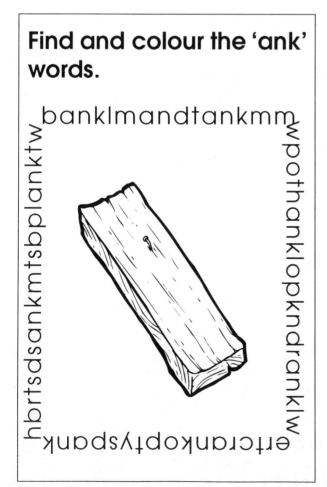

ertcrankoptyspank

hbrtsdsankmtsbplanktw

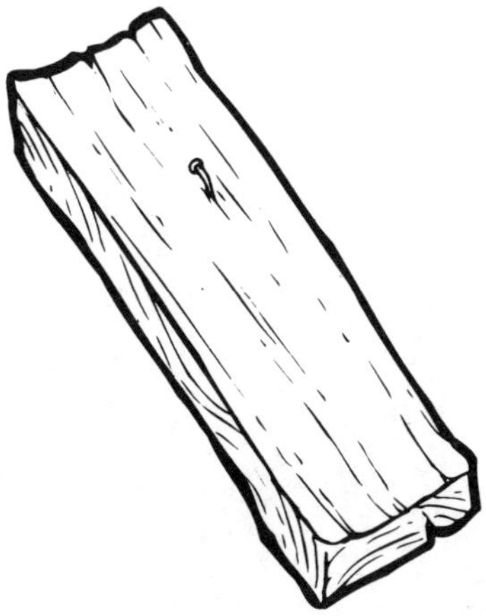

ank

drank

Match the 'ink' words to their meaning.

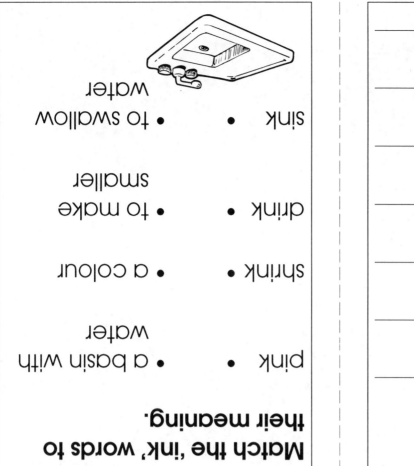

pink •	• a basin with water
shrink •	• a colour
drink •	• to make smaller
sink •	• to swallow water

Copy these words.

pink ______________

think ______________

sink ______________

twinkle ______________

shrink ______________

blink ______________

rink ______________

Circle the 'ink' words in the sentence. Draw a picture of the sentence.

'The girl with the pink dress was having a drink'

ink

think

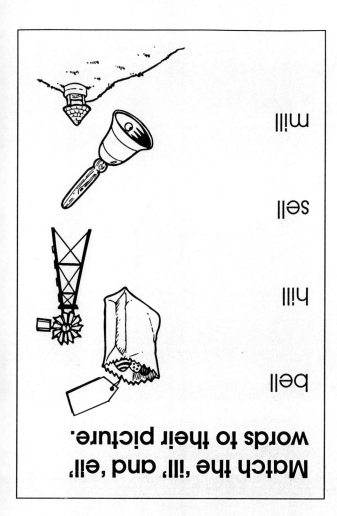

Match the 'ill' and 'ell' words to their picture.

bell

hill

sell

mill

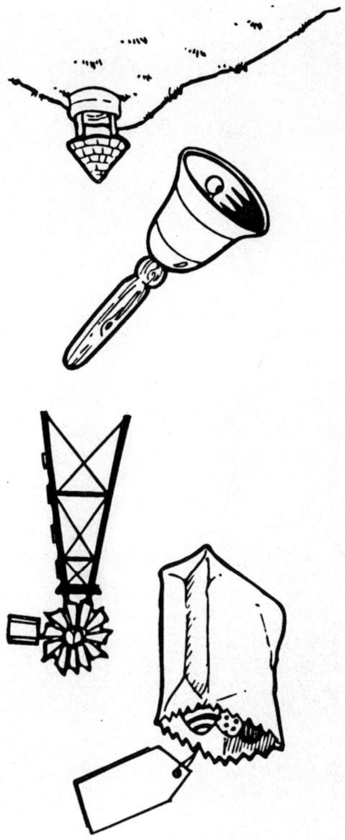

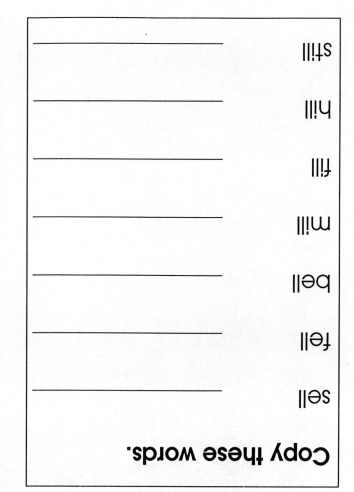

Copy these words.

sell ____________________

fell ____________________

bell ____________________

mill ____________________

fill ____________________

hill ____________________

still ____________________

Colour the correct answer.

A shell is a type of road.

Yes No

A bell makes sound.

Yes No

To sell is to buy something.

Yes No

To fill is opposite to empty.

Yes No

ill

hill

ell

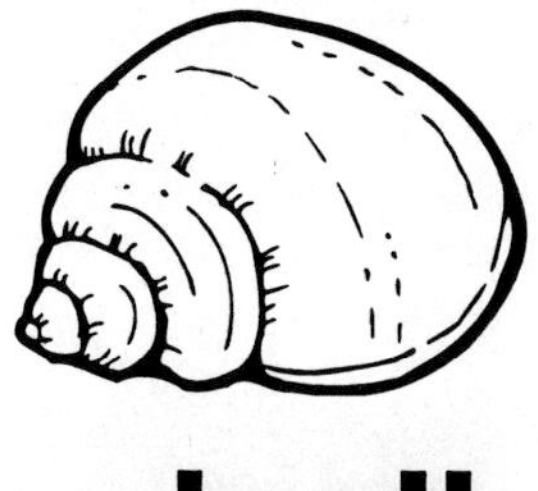

shell

Complete the 'ull' and 'oll' words.

g ull sk j - y

d oll h - y

Copy these words.

gull

skull

dull

roll

gully

jolly

holly

Complete the crossword.

gully
pull
full
doll

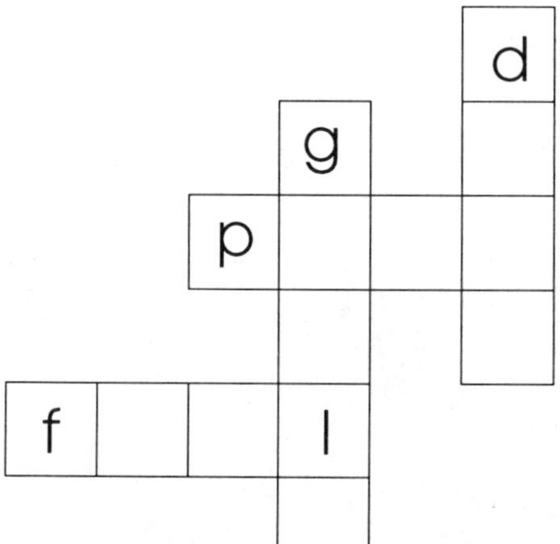

ull

gull

oll

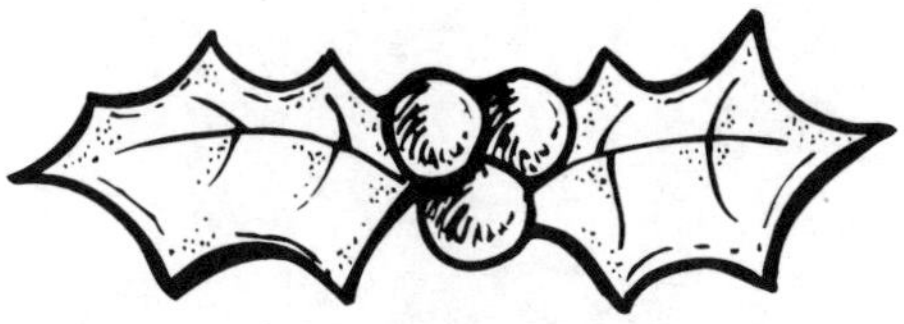

holly

Copy these words.

bold ______

old ______

fold ______

hold ______

cold ______

gold ______

told ______

Draw a picture for these words.

cold

old

Find the 'old' words.

S	O	K	A	O	L	D
O	A	B	H	P	G	L
L	M	C	O	L	T	O
D	D				G	C
O	L				G	F
A	O				O	O
A	H				L	B
I	D	L	O	F	D	O
K	J	B	C	D	O	L
T	O	L	D	E	L	D

old

gold

squ

squid

Draw a squid with a squirrel.

Copy these words.

squirt

squint

squirrel

squeal

squeeze

squash

squelch

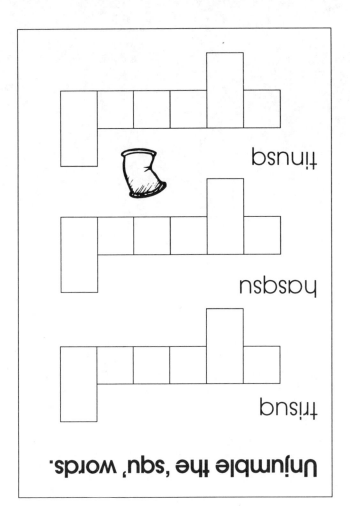

Unjumble the 'squ' words.

trisuq

hasqsu

tinusq

Complete each 'ch' words.

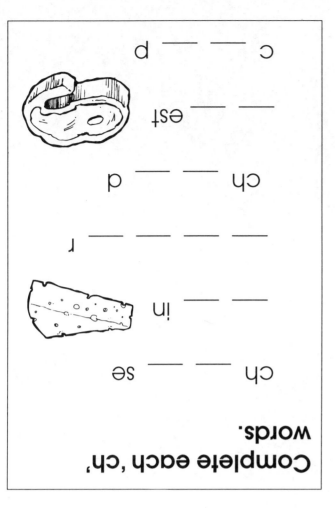

ch ___ ___ se

___ ___ in

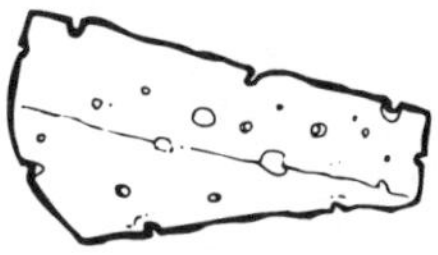

___ ___ ___ ___ r

ch ___ ___ p

___ ___ est

c ___ ___ p

Copy these words.

chin ____________________

cheer ____________________

rich ____________________

child ____________________

chest ____________________

chop ____________________

cheese ____________________

Find and colour the 'ch' words.

chinmmfgdrichmsd

rwchildmnchjilchopmns

chlchickmdcheert

mnvchscchestbncheese

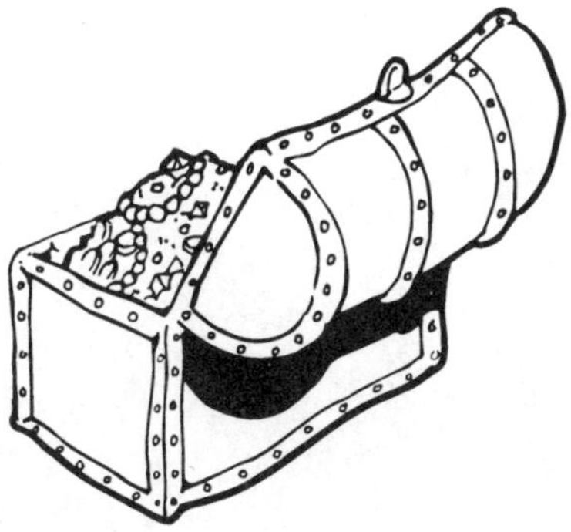

ch

chicks

Match the 'sh' words to their meaning.

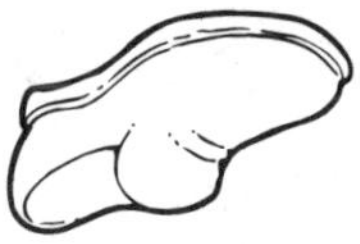

shoe •	• to complete
fish •	• worn on the foot
finish •	• opposite to open
shut •	• an animal that lives in water

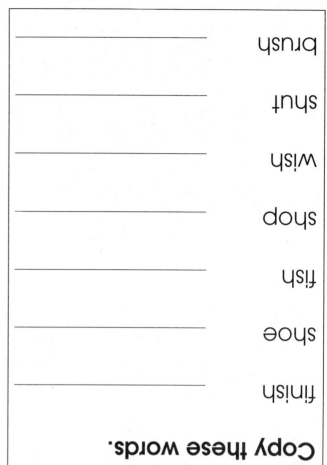

Copy these words.

finish ____________________

shoe ____________________

fish ____________________

shop ____________________

wish ____________________

shut ____________________

brush ____________________

Circle the 'sh' words in the sentence. Draw a picture of the sentence.

'The fish bought a brush from the shop.'

sh

ship

th

thief

Colour the correct answer.

Thick is the same as thin.

Yes No

A moth is a type of bird.

Yes No

A 'thud' is a type of sound.

Yes No

Thunder can happen in storms.

Yes No

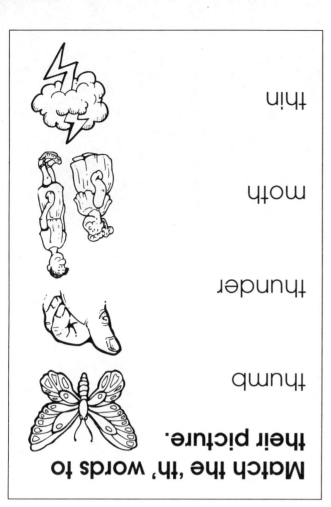

Match the 'th' words to their picture.

thumb

thunder

moth

thin

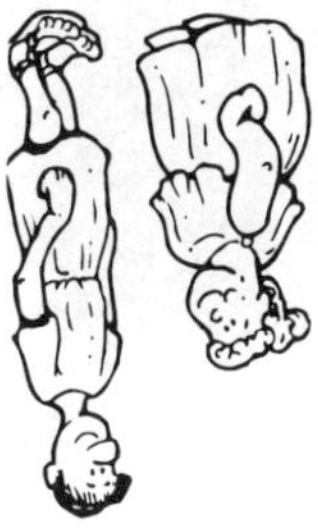

Copy these words.

thin ____________

thick ____________

thank ____________

thumb ____________

thud ____________

thunder ____________

moth ____________

wh

whale

Complete the crossword.

where
whale
whisper
wheel
whip

Copy these words.

whip ______________

where ______________

wheel ______________

whisper ______________

white ______________

wheat ______________

why ______________

Complete the 'wh' words.

ere　　wh　　eel

ite　　isper　　ale

____

____

____

____

____

ck

duck

Find the 'ck' words.

D	U	C	K	A	K	B
T	N	S	O	C	K	L
R	E	M	G	B	C	A
I	O				B	C
C	C				L	K
K	D				O	C
J	I				C	L
F	K	K	T	C	K	O
S	I	C	K	L	K	C
L	E	W	R	O	C	K

Copy these words.

black ______

sock ______

clock ______

rock ______

trick ______

block ______

sick ______

Draw a picture for these words.

trick

sock

nch

branch

Copy these words.

finch

ranch

bench

lunch

bunch

punch

crunch

Unjumble these 'nch' words.

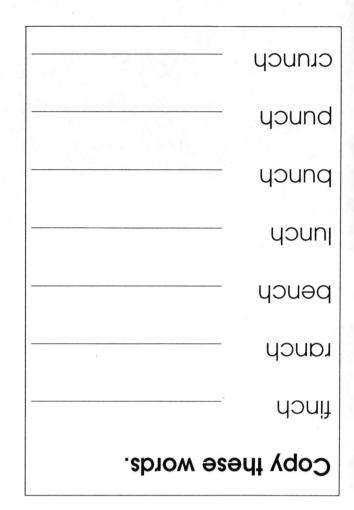

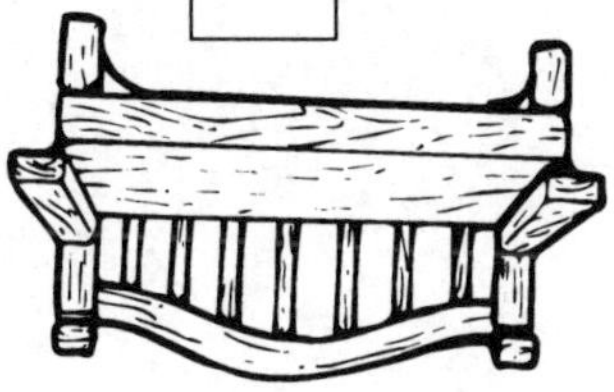

cenbh

canrh

huncp

Draw a finch on a branch.

Complete each 'tch' words.

sc ___ ___ t ___ ___

i ___ ___ h

sw ___ ___ ___ ___

st ___ ___ ___ h

___ a ___ ch

c ___ ___ ___ h

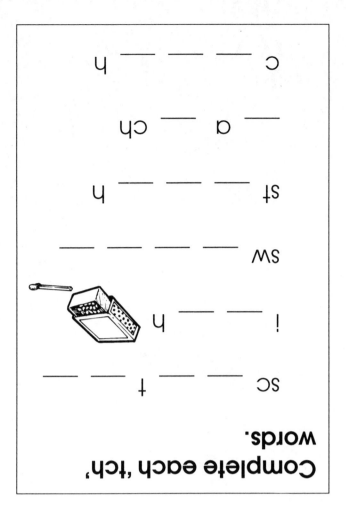

Copy these words.

hutch ____________

catch ____________

match ____________

stitch ____________

switch ____________

itch ____________

scratch ____________

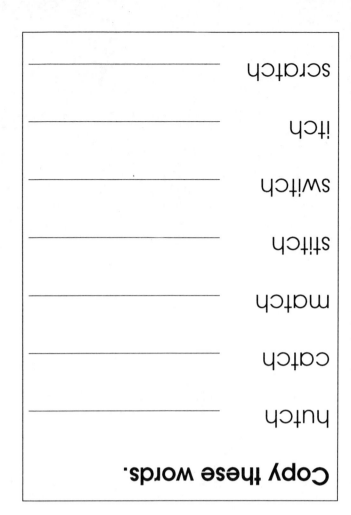

Find and colour the 'tch' words.

bmatchnsscratchm

nopwitchkklhjstitchndfal

catchoithitchfrwsa

ehutchkkhhswitchnnhysa

tch

witch

Copy these words.

hutch

catch

match

stitch

switch

itch

scratch

Complete each 'tch' words.

sc __ __ t __ __

i __ __ h

sw __ __ __ __

st __ __ __ h

__ a __ ch

c __ __ __ h

tch

witch

Find and colour the 'tch' words.

bmatchnsscratchm

catchoithitchtrwsa

thr

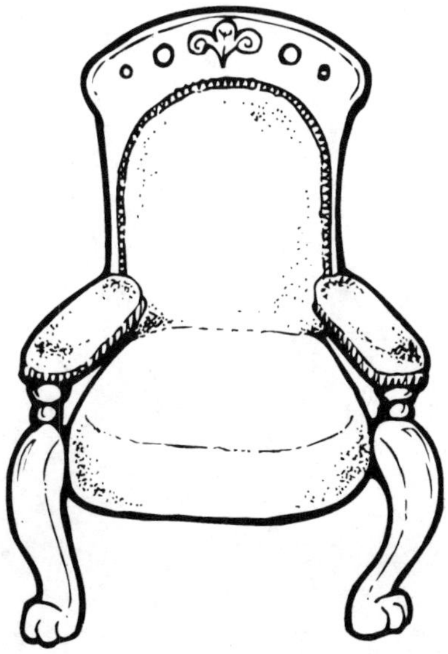

throne

Circle the 'thr' words in the sentence. Draw a picture of the sentence.

'The three children had to throw the balls through the hoop."

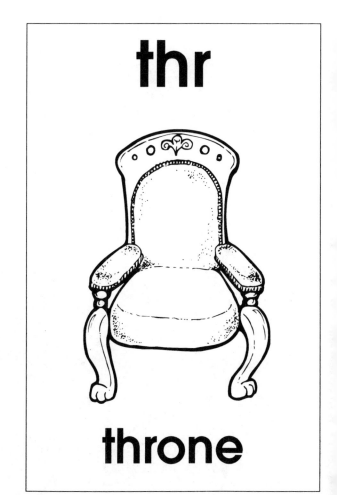

Copy these words.

thrill ____________

three ____________

thrush ____________

throat ____________

thrash ____________

throw ____________

through ____________

Match the 'thr' words to their meaning.

throw •	• the chair of a king or queen
thrash •	• to fling into the air
throne •	• a number
three •	• a part of the body
throat •	• to beat

thr

throne

Circle the 'thr' words in the sentence. Draw a picture of the sentence.

The three children had to throw the balls through the hoop.

Copy these words.

thrill

three

thrush

throat

thrash

throw

through

Match the 'thr' words to their meaning

throw •	• the chair of a king or queen
thrash •	• to fling into the air
throne •	• a number
three •	• a part of the body
throat •	• to beat

Match the 'ar' words to their picture.

tart

park

farm

sharp

Copy these words.

march ____________

tart ____________

sharp ____________

farm ____________

park ____________

mark ____________

start ____________

Colour the correct answer.

A shark lives in the water.

Yes No

A tart is a type of plant.

Yes No

Start is the opposite to finish.

Yes No

A march is a type of horse.

Yes No

ar

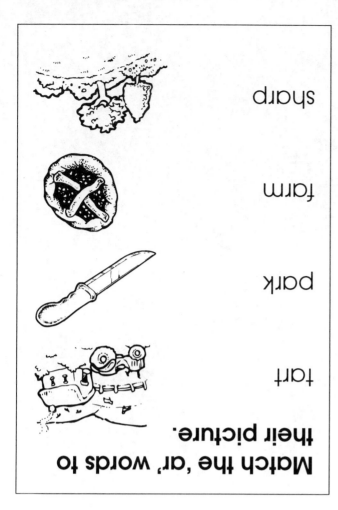

shark

Complete the 'er' words.

riv

er

ladd

clev

jump

moth

Copy these words.

river

fern

clever

gather

mother

father

jumper

Complete the crossword.

mother
father
clever
fern
river

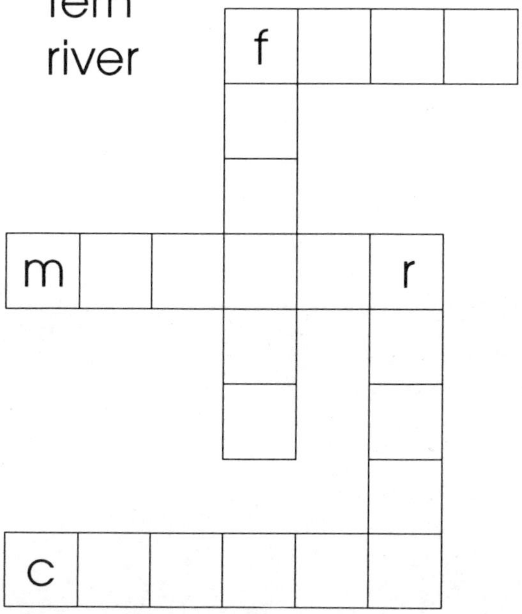

er

fern

Draw a picture for these words.

bird

skirt

Copy these words.

first

shirt

bird

third

skirt

thirst

stir

Find the 'ir' words.

F	I	R	S	T	J	G
T	R	R	D	I	C	I
H	S	K	I	R	T	R
I	T				H	L
R	I				I	R
D	R				R	B
E	C				S	I
K	S	V	I	R	T	R
B	L	H	S	C	F	D
S	H	I	R	T	A	G

ir

girl

Unjumble the 'or' words.

cohpr

corht

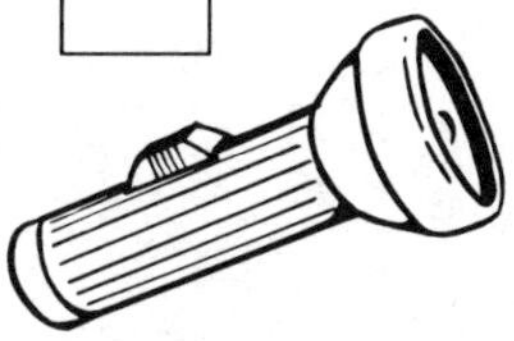

roseh

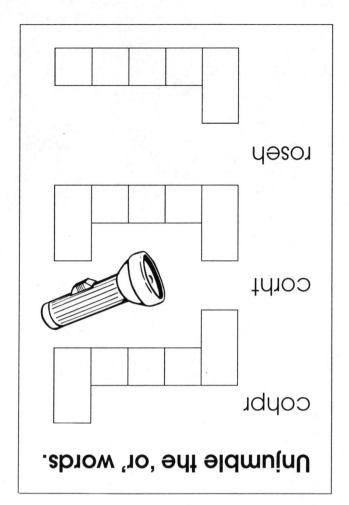

Copy these words.

porch

torch

more

cork

fork

born

thorn

Draw a fork and a torch on a horse.

or

horse

Complete each 'ur' words.

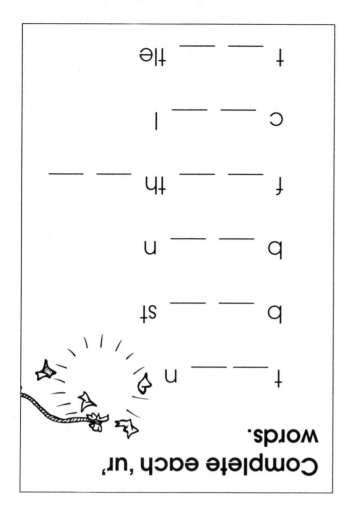

t __ __ n

b __ __ st

b __ __ n

f __ __ th __ __

c __ __ l

t __ __ tle

Copy these words.

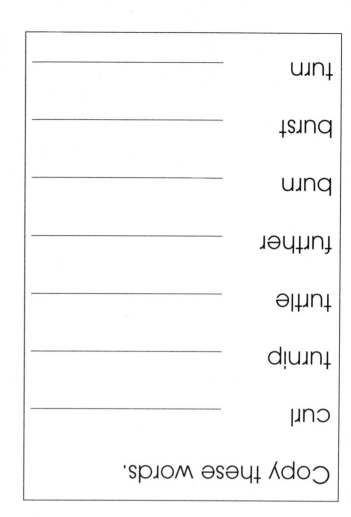

curl __________

turnip __________

turtle __________

further __________

burn __________

burst __________

turn __________

Find and colour the 'ur' words.

rsturnnbpturtlebds

gchurchrtyburstbpunvd

rsturnipmnburnmm

hdcurlnhyuorsfurthermn

ur

church

Match the 'ay' words to their meaning.

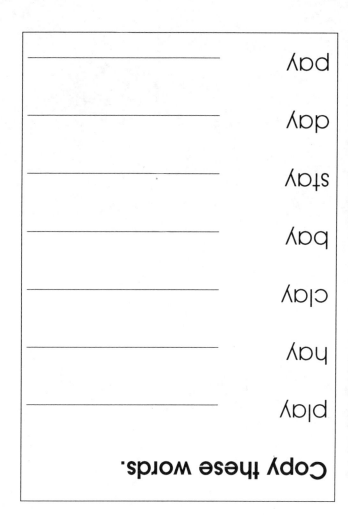

clay •	• opposite to night
pay •	• a type of earth
day •	• dried grass
hay •	• to give money for something

Copy these words.

play ________

hay ________

clay ________

bay ________

stay ________

day ________

pay ________

Circle the 'ay' words in the sentence. Draw a picture of the sentence.

'Children like to play in the hay.'

ay

bay

Match the 'ey' words to their picture.

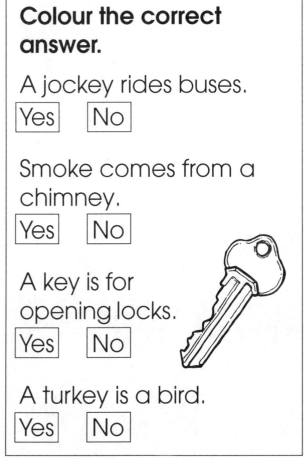

chimney

turkey

trolley

money

Copy these words.

jockey ______________________

turkey ______________________

donkey ______________________

money ______________________

chimney ______________________

key ______________________

trolley ______________________

Colour the correct answer.

A jockey rides buses.

Yes | No

Smoke comes from a chimney.

Yes | No

A key is for opening locks.

Yes | No

A turkey is a bird.

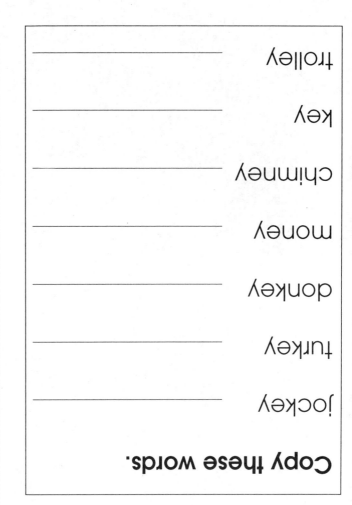

Yes | No

ey

monkey

Copy these words.

rifle

puddle

needle

little

poodle

eagle

jungle

Complete the 'le' words.

le

eag jung

need rif pudd

Complete the crossword.

poodle puddle
little beetle

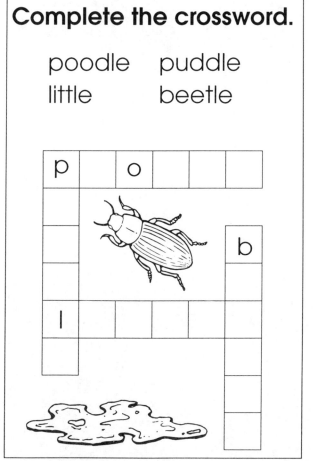

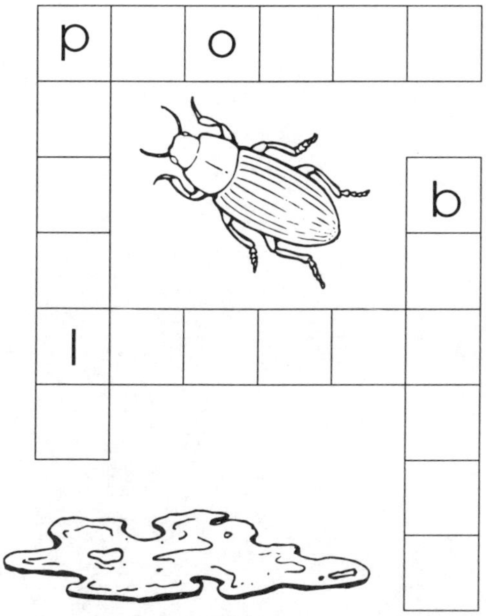

le

poodle

Draw a picture for these words.

shadow

row

Copy these words.

shadow ____________

narrow ____________

hollow ____________

slow ____________

grow ____________

know ____________

row ____________

Find the 'ow' words.

S	H	A	D	O	W	N
L	K	C	O	O	C	A
O	N	B	A	W	R	R
W	O				O	R
K	W				W	O
B	C				E	W
C	D				O	K
O	W	G	R	O	W	L
R	O	W	A	O	W	K
H	O	L	L	O	W	R

ow

crow

Copy these words.

joy

oyster

annoy

destroy

enjoy

toy

ahoy

Unjumble the 'oy' words.

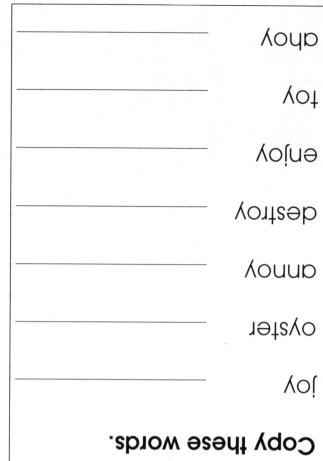

yesrot

yenjo

nnayo

Draw a boy with a toy.

oy

boy

Copy these words.

quilt ______________

quiet ______________

quick ______________

queer ______________

quite ______________

quack ______________

question ______________

Complete each 'qu' words.

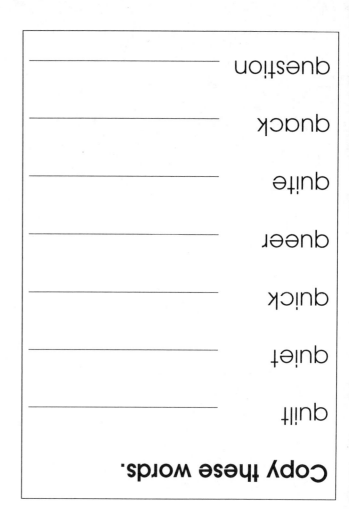

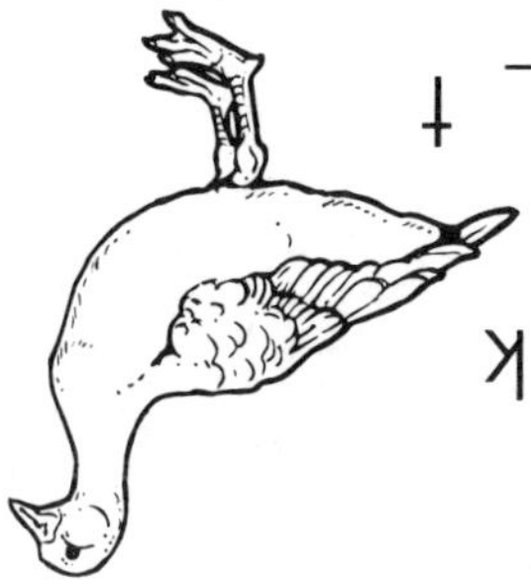

qu __ __ k

qu __ __ t

qu __ __ n

qu __ __ r

qu __ __ t

qu __ __ e

Find and colour the 'qu' words.

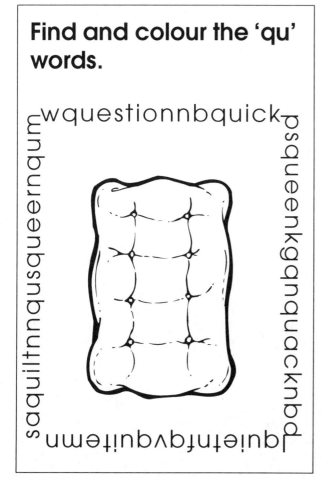

wquestionnbquick

psqueenkganquacknbd

quietnfqvquitemn

saquiltnnqusqueernqum

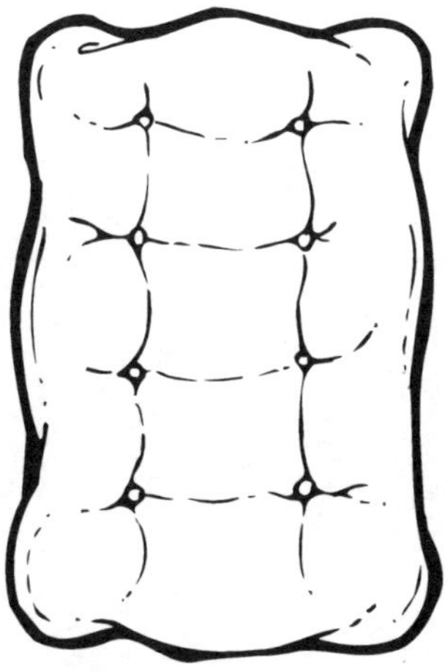

qu

queen

wa

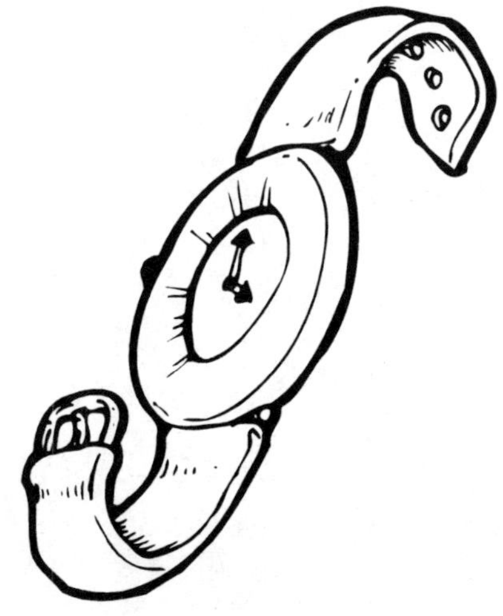

watch

Circle the 'wa' words in the sentence. Draw a picture of the sentence.

'The wasp had a wash in the water.'

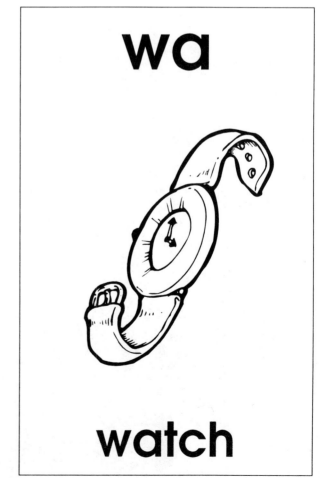

Copy these words.

wasp ____________

walk ____________

waddle ____________

wash ____________

wander ____________

wallet ____________

water ____________

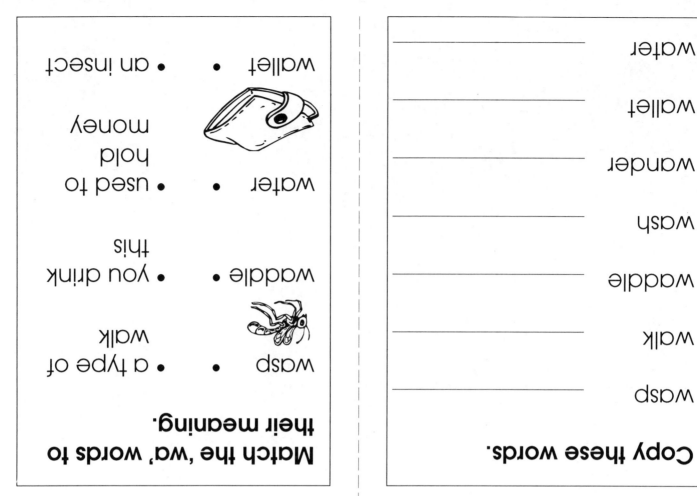

Match the 'wa' words to their meaning.

wasp •	• a type of walk
waddle •	• you drink this
water •	• used to hold money
wallet •	• an insect

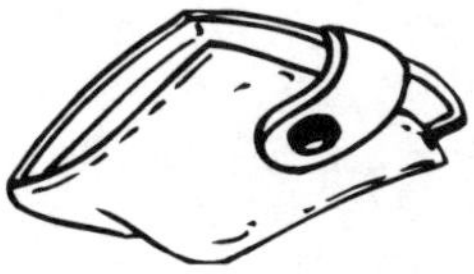